ISAAC ASIMOV'S
Library of the Universe

SATURN:
The Ringed Beauty

by Isaac Asimov

Gareth Stevens Publishing
Milwaukee

Library of Congress Cataloging-in-Publication Data

Asimov, Isaac, 1920-
  Saturn: the ringed beauty / by Isaac Asimov. -- A Gareth Stevens
children's books ed.

p.   cm. -- (Isaac Asimov's library of the universe)
  Bibliography: p.
  Includes index.
  Summary: Describes the physical characteristics, rings, moons, and
movement of the planet Saturn.
  ISBN 1-555-32389-8.   ISBN 1-555-32364-2 (lib. bdg.)
  1. Saturn (Planet) --Juvenile literature.   [1. Saturn (Planet)] I. Title. II. Series:
Asimov, Isaac, 1920-   . Library of the universe.
QB671.A85   1988
523.4'6 -- dc19   88-17563

A Gareth Stevens Children's Books edition.

Edited, designed, and produced by
Gareth Stevens, Inc. 7317 West Green Tree Road Milwaukee, Wisconsin 53223, USA

Cover painting © George Peirson
Designer: Laurie Shock
Picture research: Kathy Keller
Artwork commissioning: Kathy Keller and Laurie Shock
Project editor: Mark Sachner
Research editor: Scott Enk
Technical advisers and consulting editors: Greg Walz-Chojnacki and Francis Reddy

1 2 3 4 5 6 7 8 9 94 93 92 91 90 89

CONTENTS

Nowadays, we have seen planets up close, all the way to distant Uranus. We have mapped Venus through its clouds. We have seen dead volcanoes on Mars and live ones on Io, one of Jupiter's moons. We have learned amazing things about how the Universe was born, and we have some ideas about how it might die. Nothing can be more astonishing and more interesting.

Within our own Solar system is a world that many think is the most beautiful object we can see with our telescopes. It is the planet Saturn, with its wonderful rings. Nothing else we can see is quite like Saturn, and once you look at it, it is hard to tear your eyes away.

Let us learn something about this giant world, its brilliant rings, and its many satellites.

Isaac Asimov

A Planet with Ears?

In 1610, an Italian astronomer, Galileo (pronounced gal-ill-AY-o), became the first person to see Saturn through a telescope. It was the farthest known planet at the time, and he couldn't see it clearly. It seemed to have "ears" on each side!

Two years later, the "ears" disappeared, and Galileo was very upset.

Galileo didn't invent the telescope, but he was the first to use it for astronomy. Below left: Galileo's sketches of Saturn. The poor quality of his telescope made the rings look like "ears."

In 1655, a Dutch astronomer, Christian Huygens (HI-gens), had a better telescope. He saw that Saturn's "ears" were not really ears, but rings. The rings encircled Saturn. As Saturn went around the Sun, he saw the rings at different angles. Sometimes, he saw the rings from the side. When seen this way, they were so thin that they seemed to disappear. That was why Galileo, whose telescope was not as good, thought the rings had disappeared.

Christian Huygens improved the telescope. He could see that Saturn's "ears" were really rings.

Galileo: the man who hated "his" planet?

Saturn is named for an ancient Roman god that the Greeks called Cronus. Cronus once ruled the Universe, but was afraid his children would take his place. So each time a child was born to him, he swallowed that child. But his wife saved the youngest one, and when he grew up, he _did_ take Cronus' place. We know Galileo saw what looked like "ears" on Saturn, but then saw them disappear. Legend says he growled: "What! Does Saturn still devour his children?"

5

This picture shows how Earth would compare if we could magically place it next to
Jupiter and Saturn. Now you know why those two are called "giant planets"!

A Giant Planet

Saturn is the second largest planet in the Solar system. It is about 75,000 miles (120,000 km) across. This is about 9 1/2 times Earth's diameter. Saturn is only about one-third as massive as Jupiter. But that still leaves it 95 times as massive as Earth, and that makes it a giant planet. It is farther out than Jupiter, about 885,000,000 miles (1,416,000,000 km) from the Sun. That is 9 1/2 times as far from the Sun as we are.

At this great distance, the Sun's gravity is weak, and Saturn moves only one-third as quickly as Earth does. Moving slowly over its long trek, it takes Saturn about 29 1/2 Earth years to make one orbit around the Sun.

Even a small telescope shows that Saturn isn't quite round. Its rapid spin — more than twice that of Earth — creates the bulge.

Saturn versus Earth: the battle of the bulges

Although Saturn is much larger than Earth, it turns much more quickly on its axis — about once every 10 1/2 hours. Its middle regions thus bulge outward at the planet's equator. Earth also has a bulge, but it is much smaller. Earth is only about 13 miles (20.8 km) wider at its equator than at its poles. But Saturn is about 7,500 miles (12,000 km) wider at its equator than at its poles. So Saturn actually looks flattened when you look at it in a telescope!

A Floating Giant

Considering Saturn's size, it doesn't have much mass. If Saturn were hollow, you could pack 833 Earths into it. But Saturn has the mass of only 95 Earths. This means that Saturn must be made up of very light materials.

A cubic foot of Saturn's material would weigh, on the average, about 44 pounds (19.8 kg). This is only about 70% as much as a cubic foot of water would weigh. That means Saturn would float on water. If you could imagine putting Saturn on a vast ocean, it would float! As far as we know, Saturn is the only world that would.

Left: Unlike Earth, Saturn has no rocky surface.

If you could find an ocean big enough to put it in, Saturn would float!

A Cloudy World

Why is Saturn so light? The most common substances in the Universe are the two light gases, hydrogen and helium. Saturn is made up mostly of these gases.

When we look at Saturn through a telescope, we don't really see anything solid — just a thick, deep atmosphere. This atmosphere contains small amounts of certain substances besides hydrogen and helium. These other substances form clouds of many colors, and those clouds are the "surface" we see when we look at Saturn. Underneath the deep atmosphere, there might be a small, solid world of rock and metal.

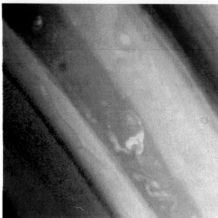

Top: Spacecraft cameras reveal details in Saturn's cloud bands. Bottom: A close-up shows twisted storm clouds and white cloud spots.

Far right: Saturn's beautiful rings arc across a sky thick with clouds. The sunlit rings seem to disappear into Saturn's shadow.

Saturn — a lightweight giant?

Despite the great differences in size and mass of the four giant planets, Jupiter, Uranus, and Neptune all have densities 1.2 to 1.7 times that of water. Only Saturn has a density less than that of water (0.7 — or 70% — of that of water). Why is its density only about half that of the other giants? We can say that Saturn has more hydrogen and helium than the others, but that does not answer the basic question: Why? Astronomers are still trying to find out.

Before space probes visited Saturn, astronomers knew of only four rings. Scientists adjusted the colors in this Voyager photo to bring out details. How many rings can you count?

The Rings — A Jewel of Nature

Saturn is surrounded by flat rings that circle its equator above its atmosphere. The rings are wide, but very thin. The brightest parts are about 45,000 miles (72,000 km) wide, but only about 500 feet (150 m) thick. This is why the rings seem to disappear when we see them sideways.

Saturn has two chief rings. These are separated by a space that was first seen by an astronomer named Giovanni Cassini. This space is called the Cassini Division. Outside the Cassini Division is the A ring. On the other side, closer to Saturn itself, is the B ring. Astronomers can make out several dimmer rings both outside and inside these two main rings.

Top: Dozens of rings circle Saturn in this Voyager 2 photo. Note the shadow of the rings on Saturn.

Left: Saturn, its rings, and the moons Tethys and Dione. The large gap in the rings is the Cassini Division.

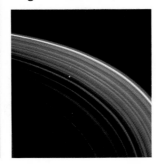

Left: The bright areas in this ring represent more matter, the dark areas less.

The planetary ring club: Why is Saturn so different?

Before 1977, we thought Saturn was the only planet with rings. But since 1977, we have discovered that the giant planets Jupiter and Uranus have rings, too. In addition, Neptune also might have a ring. When a very large planet forms, matter too close to it might not condense into satellites. But the mystery remains: Why are Saturn's rings so broad and bright, while the other planets have rings that are small, thin, and dark? Astronomers aren't sure.

?

Above: Rings thick and thin: Thousands of mini-rings make up Saturn's ring system. The F-ring, twisted by tiny moons circling nearby, is the wildest of all.

Left: Tiny ice particles above the rings bend light to give the distant Sun a "ring" of its own — a halo.

How Many Rings?

When we see Saturn's rings from Earth, they are too far away for us to see any detail. But the Voyager probes, which reached Saturn in 1980 and 1981, took care of that problem. They have shown us Saturn's rings in far more detail than ever before.

The probes showed that what look like only a few rings from Earth are really made up of many hundreds of thinner ringlets

Top: Dark "spokes" skim over Saturn's rings. Clouds of microscopic particles create the spokes by scattering sunlight.

Bottom: Two tiny moons tug Saturn's F-ring into this weird shape.

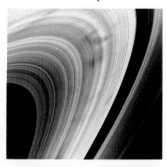

close together, with thin gaps between them. Up close, Saturn's rings look like a phonograph record!

Some of the gaps have wavy edges, and one of the ringlets is kinky. Some ringlets separate into two or three parts and appear to be braided.

The rings seem to be made up of bits of ice and rock, some as small as dust grains, and some as large as a house.

A Miniature Solar System

Saturn has at least 23 natural satellites, or moons. We might still find more.

Nine of Saturn's moons are over 120 miles (190 km) in diameter. They were discovered with telescopes on Earth. Others are tiny ones, some only about 11 miles (18 km) in diameter. These were discovered by the Voyager probes.

Saturn's moons are spread out over a huge distance. The moon closest to Saturn, Atlas, is only about 48,000 miles (77,300 km) above Saturn's cloud tops. The farthest known moon from Saturn, Phoebe, is about 6,576,000 miles (10,521,600 km) away from it. This is about 27 1/2 times farther than our Moon is from us! Saturn has the most complicated natural satellite system of any world we know!

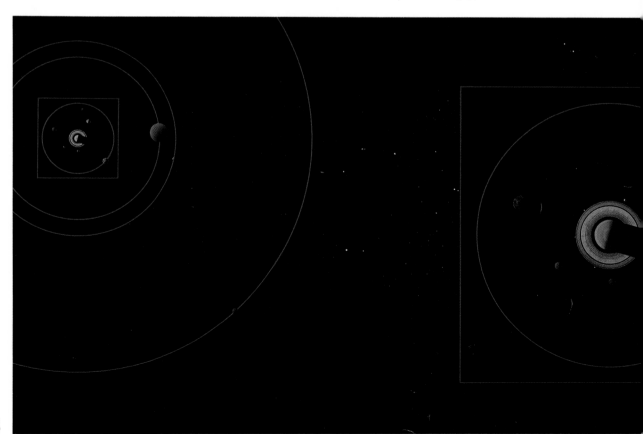

A "family portrait" of Saturn and its large moons: Dione in the foreground, Enceladus and Rhea above and to the left, Tethys and Mimas at bottom right, and distant Titan at upper right.

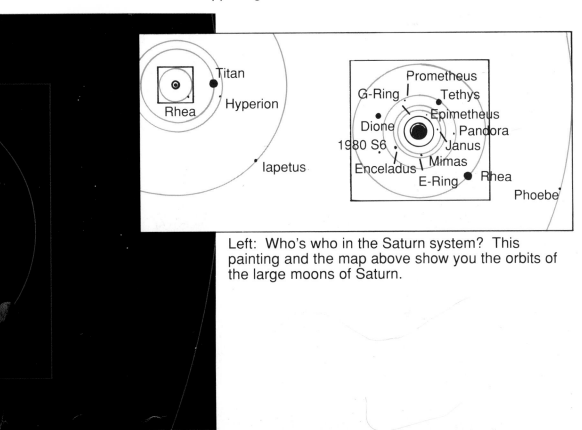

Left: Who's who in the Saturn system? This painting and the map above show you the orbits of the large moons of Saturn.

Billiard Balls and Two-toned Moons

Saturn's moons come in many varieties. Enceladus, for example, is about 310 miles (500 km) across. With its gleaming surface, this ball of ice looks as if someone had packed it into a giant billiard ball!

Iapetus, on the other hand, is about 900 miles (1,440 km) in diameter. It is the second farthest of Saturn's known moons, and it might also be a ball of ice, but it is a dirty one. Iapetus' front side, as it moves about Saturn, is dark, as if covered by dirt. But its rear side is white and shiny. It is a two-toned satellite, but astronomers still don't know why this is so.

This highly detailed picture of Enceladus was taken by Voyager 2 from 74,000 miles (119,000 km).

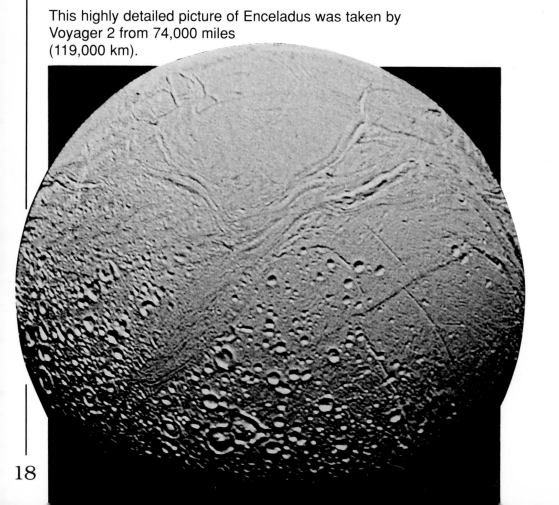

Something covers up the ice on half of Iapetus, but no one knows what it is. This painting shows what it might look like if you were standing where the moon's light and dark sides meet. Right: Iapetus as seen by Voyager 1.

Saturn's backwards moon

Phoebe is an oddball moon. The most distant of Saturn's moons, it takes about a year and a half to orbit Saturn once, but only nine hours to spin around once. Phoebe is almost three times as far away from Saturn as Iapetus, Saturn's second most distant moon. And what's more, it orbits Saturn in the direction opposite all the other moons! Why is Phoebe so different? Astronomers think it isn't an original moon at all, but a captured asteroid or comet.

Battered Satellites

The worlds of our Solar system formed when smaller pieces smashed together. Some worlds still show craters — the marks of the final pieces that struck them.

One of Saturn's moons, Tethys, is about 650 miles (1,040 km) across and has a crater that is 250 miles (400 km) across. Tethys also has a big crack in it that stretches about a third of the way around it.

Mimas, 240 miles (about 384 km) across, has a deep, round crater. The crater is about a third as wide as Mimas itself! Astronomers think that the fragment which hit Mimas almost shattered it into bits. It was lucky to survive!

Saturn rises over the rugged terrain of Rhea. The largest craters were made long ago as the moon collided with leftover fragments of ice and rock orbiting Saturn.

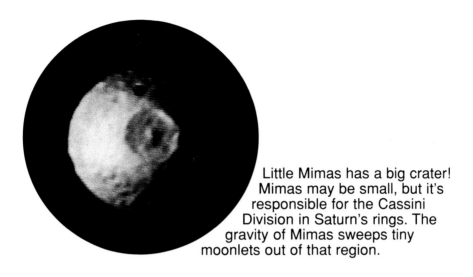

Little Mimas has a big crater! Mimas may be small, but it's responsible for the Cassini Division in Saturn's rings. The gravity of Mimas sweeps tiny moonlets out of that region.

Can you find the giant canyon of Tethys in this photo? The crack runs two-thirds of the way around the moon. Craters large and small pepper the face of Tethys.

The Small Satellites

There are five moons fairly close to Saturn, with diameters between about 20 miles (32 km) and 60 miles (97 km). They are in or near the rings. Some of them are called "shepherds," because their gravity keeps the ice grains and boulders that make up the rings from drifting too far and spreading apart. These "shepherds" keep Saturn's rings compact and bright.

There are at least two tiny moons, each about 11 miles (18 km) in diameter, that move in the orbit of Tethys. One moves ahead of Tethys, and the other stays behind it.

Another moon of Saturn, Dione, has a companion, a smaller moon called 1980 S6, that moves in Dione's orbit. Tethys and Dione are the only moons we know of that share an orbit with other moons.

Dione has a companion that plays tag! 1980 S6 orbits Saturn at the same distance. But its distance from Dione changes. Sometimes it moves closer, and sometimes farther.

Small moonlets nicknamed "shepherds" orbit near or within Saturn's rings. Their weak gravity tugs and nudges the tiny ice particles in the rings, sometimes arranging them into unusual patterns.

Did Saturn lose a moon?

In 1977, an astronomer named Charles Kowal discovered an asteroid that was much farther than any other known. He named it Chiron. It has an elliptical, or flattened, orbit, so at one end, it is a little closer to the Sun than Saturn ever gets. At the other end, Chiron is <u>twice</u> as far as Saturn is. What is an asteroid doing so far out? Maybe Chiron isn't an asteroid at all. Could it have been a satellite of Saturn that somehow got away? Astronomers don't know.

Titan's thick atmosphere is full of natural smog. Some scientists think that the smog hides a world covered with a tarlike sludge.

A Giant Satellite

By far the largest of Saturn's natural satellites, or moons, is Titan. With a diameter of about 3,200 miles (5,120 km), it is the second largest moon we know. Jupiter's moon Ganymede is a bit larger.

Titan is the only moon we know of that has a thick atmosphere. Its atmosphere is thicker than Earth's, and it is mostly nitrogen, like ours. It also contains ammonia and methane. The methane molecules clump together into larger molecules, creating smog. This smog prevents us from seeing through the atmosphere to learn what the surface is like.

Left: Titan is Saturn's largest moon. It orbits far away from the ringed planet.

Below: Tiny particles in Titan's atmosphere create a haze that keeps us from seeing its surface. This is the best view of Titan we have.

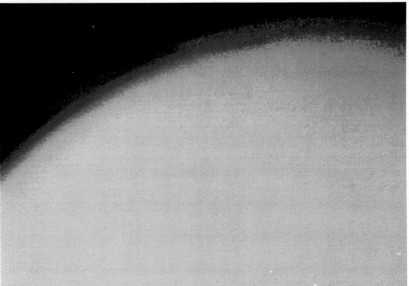

Unanswered Questions

Astronomers would love to know what Titan's surface is like. The methane in Titan's atmosphere could, under the action of sunlight, form larger molecules of tar. On Titan's solid surface of rock and ice, there might be rivers, lakes, or even oceans of liquid methane. And in these oceans, there might even be islands — or even continents — of tarry sludge.

Perhaps future probes to Saturn, and investigations with radar or with landers, can answer these and other questions. Probes might also pass through, and tell us more about, the Cassini Division. We've learned so much about Saturn in the last few years. But so many mysteries remain!

There's only one way we'll ever understand the mysteries of Saturn's moon Titan — to land on its surface. One day, spacecraft will return to Saturn. They'll launch probes into Saturn's atmosphere, and they'll launch probes to land on Titan's bizarre surface.

Fact File: Saturn

Saturn is the second largest planet in our Solar system, and the sixth closest to the Sun. Of all the outer planets, its axial tilt is the most like Earth's. A "day" on Saturn lasts only a little more than 10 1/2 hours, but since Saturn is more than 9 1/2 times farther from the Sun than Earth is, it takes Saturn much longer to orbit the Sun. In fact, a "year" on Saturn takes almost 29 1/2 of our years!

Above: The Sun and its Solar system family, left to right: Mercury, Venus, Earth, Mars, Jupiter, Saturn, Uranus, Neptune, Pluto. Right: Here is a close-up of Saturn and an assortment of its many moons.

The Moons of Saturn

Name	Atlas	Prometheus	Pandora	Epimetheus	Janus
Diameter	19 miles (30 km)	140 miles (225 km)	120 miles (193 km)	55 miles* (88 km)*	60 miles (97 km)
Distance from Saturn's Center	85,300 miles (137,248 km)	86,600 miles (139,339 km)	88,100 miles (141,753 km)	94,094 miles (151,397 km)	94,125 mi (151,447 k

Name	Mimas	Enceladus	Tethys	Calypso	Telesto
Diameter	240 miles (386 km)	310 miles (499 km)	650 miles (1,046 km)	11 miles** (18 km)**	11 miles* (18 km)*
Distance from Saturn's Center	116,962 miles (188,192 km)	149,255 miles (240,151 km)	184,284 miles (296,513 km)	185,000 miles (297,665 km)	185,000 m (297,665 k

Name	Phoebe
Diameter	120 miles (193 km)
Distance from Saturn's Center	6,576,400 miles (10,581,427 km)

Saturn: How It Measures Up to Earth

Planet	Diameter	Rotation Period (length of day)
Saturn	74,593 miles (120,020 km)	10 hours, 39 minute
Earth	7,926 miles (12,756 km)	23 hours, 56 minute

The Sun and Its Family of Planets

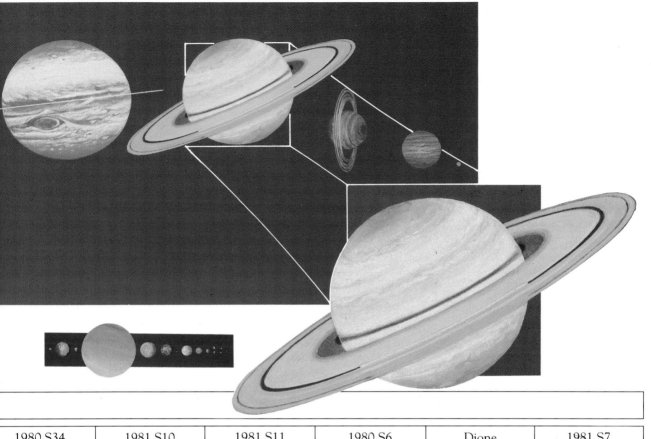

1980 S34	1981 S10	1981 S11	1980 S6	Dione	1981 S7
11 miles** (18 km)**	11 miles** (18 km)**	11 miles** (18 km)**	100 miles (161 km)	700 miles (1,126 km)	11 miles** (18 km)**
205,000 miles (329,845 km)	205,000 miles (329,845 km)	220,000 miles (353,980 km)	235,300 miles (378,598 km)	235,557 miles (379,011 km)	236,000 miles (379,724 km)

1981 S8	1981 S9	Rhea	Titan	Hyperion	Iapetus
11 miles** (18 km)**	11 miles** (18 km)**	950 miles (1,529 km)	3,190 miles (5,132 km)	890 miles (1,432 km)	220 miles* (354 km)*
236,000 miles (379,724 km)	290,000 miles (466,610 km)	327,992 miles (527,739 km)	758,998 miles (1,221,227 km)	933,514 miles (1,502,024 km)	2,211,800 miles (3,558,786 km)

* Diameter at widest point   ** Estimated diameter

Period of Orbit Around Sun (length of year)	Moons	Surface Gravity	Distance from Sun (nearest-farthest)	Least Time It Takes for Light to Travel to Earth
29.46 years	at least 23	1.19✦	844-944 million miles (1.35-1.51 billion km)	1.1 hours
365.25 days (1 year)	1	1.0✦	92-95 million miles (147-152 million km)	—

✦ Multiply your weight by this number to find out how much you would weigh on this planet.

More Books About Saturn

Here are more books that contain information about Saturn. If you are interested in them, check your library or bookstore.

Our Solar System. Asimov (Gareth Stevens)
Planets. Barrett (Franklin Watts)
The Planets. Couper (Franklin Watts)
Saturn: The Spectacular Planet. Branley (Crowell Jr. Books)
Solar System. Lambert (Franklin Watts)

Places to Visit

You can explore Saturn and other parts of the Universe without leaving Earth. Here are some museums and centers where you can find a variety of space exhibits.

NASA Lyndon B. Johnson Space Center
Houston, Texas

NASA Goddard Space Flight Center
Greenbelt, Maryland

Edmonton Space Sciences Centre
Edmonton, Alberta

Hayden Planetarium
Boston, Massachusetts

NASA Lewis Research Center
Cleveland, Ohio

Lawrence Hall of Science
Berkeley, California

National Museum of Science and Technology
Ottawa, Ontario

Dow Planetarium
Montreal, Quebec

For More Information About Saturn

Here are some people you can write to for more information about Saturn. Be sure to tell them exactly what you want to know about or see. Remember to include your age, full name, and address.

For information about Saturn:
National Space Society
600 Maryland Avenue SW
Washington, DC 20024

The Planetary Society
65 North Catalina
Pasadena, California 91106

Space Communications Branch
Ministry of State for Science
    and Technology
240 Sparks Street, C. D. Howe Building
Ottawa, Ontario K1A 1A1 Canada

About planetary missions:
Jet Propulsion Laboratory
4800 Oak Grove Drive
Pasadena, California 91109

NASA Kennedy Space Center
Educational Services Office
Kennedy Space Center, Florida 32899

Alabama Space and Rocket Center
Space Camp Applications
One Tranquility Base
Huntsville, Alabama 35807

Glossary

asteroid: a miniature planet of the Solar system, also called a minor planet or a planetoid. Most asteroids orbit the Sun between the planets Mars and Jupiter.

astronomer: a scientist who studies bodies in the Universe beyond Earth.

atmosphere: the gases surrounding a planet, star, or moon.

axis: the imaginary straight line on which a planet, star, or moon rotates.

Cassini Division: the space between the two major rings of Saturn. It is named for Giovanni Cassini, the Italian scientist who first saw this space.

comet: an object made of ice, rock, and gas. It has a vapor tail that may be seen when the comet's orbit is close to the Sun.

continents: large bodies of land found on Earth.

crater: a hole in the ground caused by a meteor strike or volcanic explosion.

cubic foot: the amount of space contained in a real or imaginary cube one foot (0.3 m) high, one foot long, and one foot wide.

density: the amount of something in a unit measured by its volume. Saturn has a density less than that of water.

diameter: the length of a straight line through the exact center of a circle or sphere. Saturn has a diameter of about 75,000 miles (120,000 km).

equator: an imaginary line around the middle of a planet that is always an equal distance from the two poles of the planet. The equator divides the planet into two half-spheres, or hemispheres.

Galileo: an Italian scientist who, in 1610, became the first to see Saturn through a telescope.

gravity: the force that causes objects like the Sun and its planets to be attracted to one another.

helium and hydrogen: two light gases that are the most common substances in the Universe.

Huygens, Christian: the Dutch astronomer who, in 1655, first identified Saturn's rings.

mass: a quantity, or amount, of matter.

matter: a particular kind of substance or the material that makes up something. For example, Saturn's ring matter includes particles of ice.

molecules: the smallest particles of a substance.

probe: a craft that travels in space, photographing celestial bodies and even landing on some of them.

radar: the use of radio waves to detect distant objects and learn their location and speeds.

rings: the bands of ice, rock, and dust particles that circle some planets, including Saturn, at their equators.

satellite: a smaller body, such as a moon, orbiting a larger body, such as a planet.

"shepherds": small moons, or moonlets, that orbit within or near Saturn's rings. Their weak gravity helps keep ring matter from drifting out of position.

Solar system: the Sun, planets, and all the other bodies that orbit the Sun.

terrain: land or ground.

Index

The publishers wish to thank the following for permission to reproduce copyright material: front cover, p. 24, © George Peirson, 1988; p. 4 (upper), The Granger Collection, New York; pp. 4 (lower left), 17 (lower right), © Laurie Shock, 1988; p. 5 (upper), AIP Niels Bohr Library; p. 5 (lower), British Museum; pp. 6, 10 (upper), 13 (all), 17 (upper right), 18, 19 (lower), 21 (lower), 22, 24, 25 (lower), courtesy of NASA; p. 7 © Kurt Burmann, 1988; pp. 8-9, © Lynette Cook, 1988; p. 9 (lower), © Tom Miller, 1988; pp. 10 (lower), 12, 15 (upper right, lower right), 21 (upper), Jet Propulsion Laboratory; pp. 11, 14, © John Foster, 1988; pp. 14-15, © Larry Ortiz, 1988; pp. 16-17, © George Peirson and Debra Peirson, 1988; p. 19 (upper), © Michael Carroll, 1984; p. 20, © Joe Tucciarone; p. 23, © Julian Baum, 1988; p. 25, © Paul Dimare, 1988; p. 26, © Brian Sullivan, 1988; pp. 28-29 (large), © Sally Bensusen, 1987; p. 29 (small), © 1988, Sally Bensusen.